*o*varian *t*wists
new and selected poems

An*yssa* **K**i*m*

Fly By Night Press
a subsidiary of *A Gathering of the Tribes, Inc.*

Ovarian Twists, New & Selected Poems by Anyssa Kim
© 2003
All rights reserved
Printed in the United States of America

Library of Congress Cataloging-in-Publication Data
Kim, Anyssa.
Ovarian Twists / new & selected poems by Anyssa Kim. -1st ed.
ISBN 1-930083-02-5

Fly By Night Press
  a subsidiary of A Gathering of the Tribes, Inc.
P.O. Box 20693
New York, NY 10009
Tel: (212) 674-3778   Fax: (212) 388-9813
E-mail: info@tribes.org   Website: www.tribes.org

Book Design & Layout: *Joe DeVito III*
Artwork on Front & Back Covers • Inside Illustrations: *Anyssa Kim*
Photos of Front & Back Cover Art • Author's Photo: *Nikki Johnson*

Produced at The Print Center, Inc. 225 Varick St., New York, NY 10014, a non-profit facility for literary and arts-related publications. (212) 206-8465

Acknowledgments

I would like to thank all of those who helped to make this book possible:

Thank you, Steve Cannon for all your support and mentorship, and for truly believing in me. Thanks to Luis for the introduction that made it all happen. Special thanks to Erick for what must be left unsaid.

Thank you Nikki and Joe, for your hard work and artistic synergy.

Thanks to Ishle, Edwin, Peter, Amy, Melanie, Yuko, Cynthia, and Maya. Plus a huge thank you to all my friends who have shown incredible support and patience throughout the process of getting this book together.

Table of Contents

*dedicated to
the woman
who gave birth to me*

*thank you for finally showing yourself to me
in my dreams*

medusa

01

today my hair swells
  a little too untamed
not interested
  in entertaining
iron-skinned visitors

i tell them:
you should not have come
and they drop down
beg me on knees not to
remove their hands from eyes

those who i let go
back to familiar darkness
always return

each man melting into
another wave
lapping
  at sand
frightened of anemones
  in a cold soup where

they do not know time
  intimately as i do—

the way of lovers
  who have embraced
on salty rocks   eroding
  anything of matter

>>

time, my sole companion
      treasure men want
to steal   but never able
to keep—

so instead,
     i offer to keep
 them

man, why do you always
want it both ways,
conjuring up
contingency plans
that your brothers
might rescue you
from your own desire

will you ever decide?
no, you are more like
apollo's lost child
jumping over shadows
of the sundial

do not bring
any more bribes here—
      they are unwanted
same as your
manifest desire, how it eclipses
    before gazing upon my face
    turn, you   from
the single moment
      of truth so coveted

go on!
unsheathe your virile sword
drawn out of
    repulsion

attempt to reclaim
your reputation
        woman smiter
you are no different
than the ones before,
those who tried in vain
to conquer themselves
through me

shrouds

the dead don't worry over
trivial vestments adorned
by the living. only
the upright need garments
as consolation to shield unsure selves
from howling winds of truth.
and so encumbered, they mask the deceased
in their image, prior to burial.
but spirits wear history as patches sewn
over vacant eyes. they moan
beneath canons of birds and volcanoes
choked on ashes of eternity.
their only links to the living rest
on diminished sighs fallen in
the dry cup of afterthought.

green acorns

> like dilapidated houses,
> lost within fragments of a neighborhood—
> night floods down upon
> each painted life, peeling,
> depreciating, nostalgic.

july

stab my brain
wake it up

the warm ooze
of yesterday
was something else

entirely of course

his bangs hung low
over eyes

didn't want me to
see his thoughts
how bright they were

how considerate

how bung
to use hair
as lampshade

summer evening
breeze kisseds
f our eyelids

bright lights
attract moths

maybe that's why
I like him

plunge

07

how easel

take a dab of

lovelust

eight-letter-dirty-word-compounded

sheds heat
presses my knees
together
to hold it in
so I don't forget

caveman hair *yank*
lessons
on Darwin, Freud
got laid on white sheets
for all to read

be my teacher
I   want   to   play   hooky
and be real bad
it's what I like to do

I know how you like to get erect
pupils

No!   now I turn woman
wet with exclamation
point howls   in loud vowels

oh *baaaaa*by!!!

my red crescent parts in
waves
caught by   cotton
cloud on a string
flies high   nestled in   thigh-sky
shangri-la, inside
man-made synthetic g-string   vibrations

pull it outta me
and burrow in
oh bloody hell
smack me so I don't forget
my animal side
inside   and   outside
runs wild
circles
eight-letter-dirty-words
up and down
us

photograph of you

some people I've met
were superstitious
believed their souls could get
captured by photographs
those shutter clicks
    click   click   click
clack sounds of up
and down jaw
stiff rubber gum
between teeth sticks
cavity fillings loose
saliva stretches strain
more flavor, more flavor
but the brightness of the
moment that first moment
when the gum squirts the
tongue is no more, and
the moment I keep
searching for, somewhere
on that tongue why
don't I just spit it out
it's dead already
been dead for hours
and   click click click
I blink maybe in some
corner of my mind in
my DNA maybe I believe
those folk superstitions
must somehow be true as

the shutter clicks of my
small suspicious eyes never fully
remember you
just before that blink
     just before that   click click
you are different
and I strain to see you as before
keep you there
you keep moving
and changing while I strain to
keep up but
maybe that gum
flavor of you is still on my tongue
so let me take that picture
before you change again

almost

I could paint him
a thousand times
and still never know
his skin

at his age
I couldn't have appreciated
the singular beauty
of such angles

I could cross his path
every day and yet
he'd never see

the television at home
entertains
an empty chamber

digital marionettes with
eyes follow closely,
accusing
across the room
back and forth
                the remote remains untouched
back and forth
and back

they mock
happy ending after
happy ending,
happily ever after

I sit, alone, flat
on the opposite side of the set
watch the clock
as the future arrives
in spasms

I remember
his jaw sharp as his

tipped nose
pensive, at the rumble
beneath his worn
loafers

remembering,
relieving myself of those
still images,
so many singulars
haunting each moment

diary entry

I've entered you
propped up
inside hot
circular wind
of diagonal stings. You
distant, lean.
breathe out
long toils etched in a
sheen,
groove. heatly.
        And rosy cheeks,
so richly. Touches
your mama artisan
        created.
in her dream palace
        —perpendicular
her masterpiece
        beheld. some.
in her hand. some.
        a while—
        papa was mad. some.
of the many. he
who lives in your smile
when glass breaks
        windows of your mama's eyes
images of you. swan. gliding on her sorrow
        my ripples
        break reflections
of a dream sky above,
        where she used to go
        carrying a single flame.

dated

last pot of ideas
run dry   its heat
consumed by
thirsting

steeped
full of hurry   you
rise steam   and
bolt   leave only
a breeze—

parting   your pseudo
lingered kiss
sears past   unwet

coat flaps behind
you run   its
material tongue
licks up distance
between us

giant teeth buildings
snarl   from sky face
at two   jack
hammering   feet
beat

outside the glass eye
i am left to ponder
old news
you left
on the table

four a.m.

beginning is the end is the

closing

napkins. illegible scribble

don't. under. stand. help.
under. stand. me. under.
don't. help. stand. me.
under. me. don't. stand.
help?

waiter no
spekee dee englishee

I. speak. clear. ly.

I. peak. sclear. ly.

I. leak. spear. cly.

I. cleak. slear. ply.

I. squeak. pleak. ry.

one language.
one languor.
one linguor.
one liquor.

slur. blur.
one hundred proof. in the pudding.

gotsa light? darkit'smoky in here.

deposit

i wait to make my
deposit
in line   the bank
 d o t t e d line
impatient

there are ghosts
  between   me
and the   next

we wait
together

a wall clock ticks
its arms
move through seconds

the customer ahead
his stomach
growls

chinese food next door
teases

ghosts are hungry too
they sigh

we all wait together

for the teller bell

oblivio
  us

the ticking

Obviously you don't. Yes, the ticking, that's right.
Yes, I understand you don't. Hear the ticking. Does
it annoy you?

No, not that kind of ticking. Not a left-to-right
ticking. Nothing sequential or linear like that. One
tick doesn't follow the other like how you're doing it.
Not up and down either. No. More like,
more...*circular*. Yes, that's it. Circular ticking. No I
can't give you an example. I couldn't even try to
imitate it.

Of course I realize how strange that sounds. Circular
ticking does indeed sound strange. Yes, I realize
that's not how you meant. You didn't understand.
You don't. No, I didn't mean it that way.

It's like how you're causing static in my head right
now. Yes, that's right. Black and white snow hissing
in my television brain. Sure I can see it. No I can't
point it out to you. Well, because *that's* how I see my
thoughts running, from the inside-out, behind my
eyeballs, while you and everyone else plant tires all
over the obstacle course of my mind. Hundreds—
perhaps even thousands—of them at once, every
second. Major interference. A myriad ignorant,
malicious crows sitting atop one fragile wire.

Dr. Campbell? No, I haven't seen Dr. Campbell in
a while. Between you and me, I think Doc was once a
mental patient a long time ago—at least that's what I
heard through the grape wine. It would explain those
gynecological exams on the black leather couch.
Squeak.

Big smile. Big hanging teeth. "Open. Wide." Oh
yes, I remember riding through the Grand Canyon.

I always hated stirrups, especially without spurs.
Faux cowboy. Eat meat. I'm a cow-person. Half-
and-half Grade-A ground beef. Where is it, baby?
Take a look while my knees scissor the sky as I slide
through it. I'm slick as sludge.

I can hear your thoughts ticking. Tick, tick, tick. Yes,
I can see them too. A straight line riding off into the
sunset, searing all the clouds in its path, shrill as an
echolalia yodel. I'm a Swiss Miss with
marshmallows! A Yankee Doodle noodle riddled with
Bovine Spongiform Encephalopathy!
Cock-a-doodle-*moo*.

Yes, it's noon, so rise and shine with me—up, up and
roll away inside my shopping cart mind rolling down
the supermarket aisle of experience. Upon
professional recommendation I now collect and pay
later on the government subsidized propaganda
program called "Charge-A-Life." I'll always chop off
a good ear to heartfelt advice. Of *course* I'll bring
home the Campbell's.

Tick tock. The pills are pink. I'm dreaming about
your pendulum. It's a guillotine. I fancy we bring
out the best in each other, don't we.

Hey Dr. Campbell...er, *Mom*? Is our session up yet?

after the rain

little spitz
my fluffy white snow sneeze
with mud boots
mama didn't mean to
kick you
some broken petunias
must have possessed her shoe
but how could our simplicity
comprehend the significance
of a tended garden
we can misunderstand together
domestication of all things small
me, by sceptre of wooden spoon
and the broom we both know
since we always forget how
hard she works to sweep clean
broken remnants of her day
perfection achieved by 5:12
on the dot dad must be
presented with an old world model
of all things orderly and good,
while we tremble
together, under the kitchen table
for whatever ground we brought in
from outside

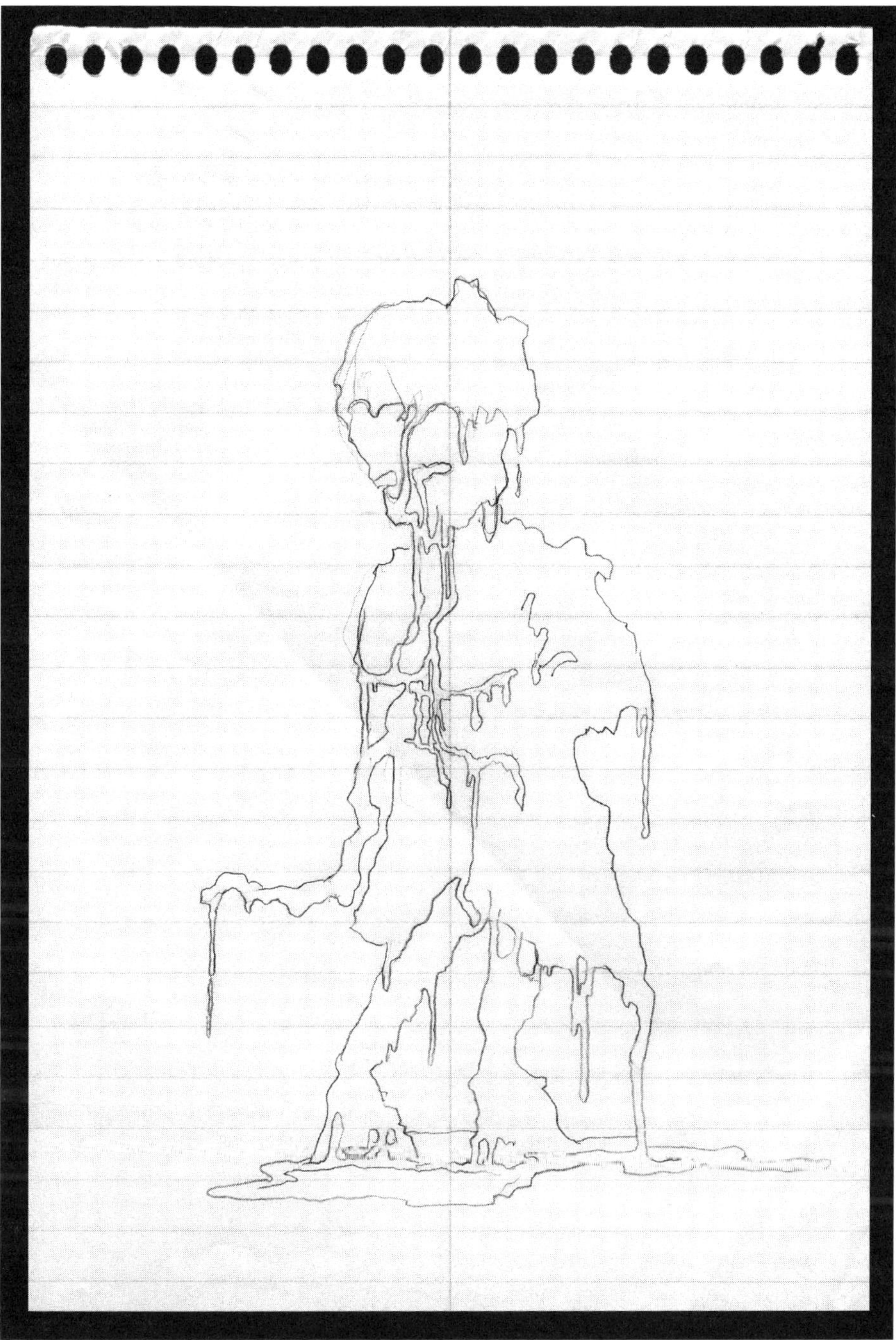

winter triptych

they never hear me calling through the thick of
winter. he, bent over dead grass as if his shadow
could call it back from dying. and mama in the
kitchen communing with the dead lamb. but the
man bent over not her husband/ he a river of shade
defying heavy light pouring down over his grief.
caws of crows in the distance/ shout in response to
the muted clangings of his heart as/ his fists clench
to ignore the aroma of slaughter wafting through my
hair. i am silent, an angel keeping his feet heavy on
the ground, breathing in the water of his tremors.
his tears sink into soil as she continues to stir stew,
her alchemy grips his throat so he cannot scream.
yet he hovers. and hovers. she smiles thinly/ as i fly
away with the crows, up and crash through slate
clouds, broken to millions of hard chips falling over
his back.

mutably exclusive

would the widow
ever wish to return
to the lips
of her first kiss,
risking sacrilege

    must expectation
    always accumulate
    old laundry
    in the hourglass

tales so often woven
around pupa's
morph to imago
struggle of crawler
into winged angel

    today i wonder
    of the tattered chrysalis
    where none yet
    pay homage

how effectively
growth   inherent
sufferance
has wooed
temporal
amnesia
to its sheets

    in hangnails of home
    in falling of bridges

longitude (east)

mother, you are

the missing twin

the ghost limb

and i've become like you,

forgetting

        where i've been

how cold the air, crystalline

icicles collar the heart

        i never thought i'd grow any,

but genetics are shackles in

repetition, to resemble you

        that day you walked away

to let another woman take your place

you should have taken your scent with you

fragrance of the east, whose phantom

lingers over unformed lips that can never

utter your name,

a spirit that cannot be exorcised

remains,

senseless and malformed

as the toes of ancient

chinese concubines

and now, as you bend through

the remaining shadows of your life

i see the world through your eyes,

small and dark,

where beneath a cold spring's surface

tree roots never touch

and crabgrass sucks the earth dry

to simply grow and die

anonymous

prologue to *Sarah*

they of big hands and block jaws
grabbed the schoolgirl by the hair
threatened to smack her good
if she didn't stop
crying so loud

i've seen those hands   as if
they were calloused feet
            following me
from life to life
from sleep to wake

she carries my slouch
though she hasn't yet
even reached
puberty

    her folds turn over
inside, origami twists
    and layers
where she hides herself

until night
when her hands grow feathers
flapping away at bad dreams
            flying
out the window

bod mod

blade, beautiful silver
french kiss flesh
drink up ruby slippers
blood tongue twister

faceless blade, careless
who cares? not
whose hand cuts. flesh
does not care

scarlet,
my pretty   is not
    caring

          art
does not

    why do you, face-
 less
          beast?

jitters

i am playing piano • hear each note • is • a • word •
plummet spackles of body language art hangles •
dangles *there* ridiculing me through lightwaves •
clashes of anticolors i cannot harmonize • song of
vulnerability fully exposed • exposure x-rayed in
triple x marks the bench they sit • y judge dancing in
pews is laughing • stabbed skin crawls in and out
bubbles ready to burst red balloon rising below
ceiling • i want to page turn out • window out •
wrong notes *out* of stutter blanks to • *stay put* •
sputters of greased me over microphone • phone is
ringing • bells crashing in ears there is slippage •
slip slidage all over sound system crashing through •
lipped barriers of logic • too dangerous to associate
with free association • hands shake • steady now •
we are ready • let's play • plunkage •

gypsy airs

I am   a   rising gypsy skirt
     see saw violin   slide up scale
legs of   blooming, circular, tips   around

                    dance   of the   Pernambuco
          lost forests of distant   rainbows   the arc of
finger stretch   out the caravan   *come closer*

light wanders   past   drunken dust
        oh the mouths they are   so open
g-clefs   f l y   up sleeves   beneath shoes

the   music   has only
     just begun

SOB's

drums impervious to palms
drunken beats flog
the heels of dancers
to resemble jesters
in ridiculous gyrations

the office has taken a vacation
we celebrate in baths of sweat
copulate cigarette smoke
as it fingers our hair

women's feet dance lighter
leaps sprung from toes
perhaps to compensate
the weight of their ovaries

men agog at bare thighs
feign nonplus in oak rigidity
tequila shots the cure-all
to flaccidate inhibitions

some seem too old to be here
but the primal is ageless
ancestors summoned from
sleep deep in bone
through tranced skin
traces, perceptible in
the timeless movement of storm

music lesson

32

he taught music shines
  through every color
so I never saw him as a black man
rather, someone like me,
my teacher, whom God had poured
melted Hershey's over
leaving the rest of school
vanilla pudding

the bellies of his hands
were hued a light tan
they must have been
shadowed from the sun
though I'd been blinded by it
that is how my chiseled eyes
saw our world,

the one I'd race to
down the corridor
past chemical odors
of the custodian, whose
big block capital letters
held no "Mister" before it,
and no name after

but he, he was Mr. Vance

his name, hung with importance

upon door opened to

wide Cheshire smile,

a simple flash of brilliance

hovered over proud barrel chest

covered in sweaters, scratchy,

like the flat tones he'd gently correct

bidding them "higher, higher"

demonstration of his life

passion, crescendoed,

as he played violin

with heavy vibrato

in that room

he made me want to

sing my wood

in the same timbre as his

wynton's jazzy hornétude

34

there is a man tap dancin
up the mountain, the metal
mountain, tap tappin to
the sky thru his fingers

can't sit still   there are
feet moving me thru
my seat a bam boom
shoe percussion

the tap man got a trumpet
horn blarin out his cheeks
he climbs that mountain
on his trumpet feet

fly and jump there's a
slip slip slip slide
atop the lily lip pond
the gold man sings

cascades of syncopation
make the cool man sweat
even light overhead
wants to belt a tune
in time   with hue

crammed and bouncin
beneath red-white-n-blue
umbrellas we swing
grab the tonic now that
you're   here
            this is living
this is serious   playing
            this is no

                        returning

pop

Don't spill those bubble thoughts too heavy or they may drop from
the rise of sunskate over my head like mercury conspiring in white
against the blue backdrop. Don't you hear? *Shhhh.* Spread it and
sweat ascends tree buckets a spire high up to the heavens. Don't you
see me fly daddy, don't you see. Don't you see me. Knees ache from
the back and forth, the back and forth. Rocking tree horse of wood
tree spire, cunt spires, don't you see me rocking, me little girl. Oh
daddy oh daddy ohdaddy*ohhhdaddy*.

No you were never there and I was too ugly for you to wanna fuck
me, weren't I daddy-o. Men and again with backs of prickly hair
porcupiney, rubbed through porcine alibis. No cherry pie, no
goodbyes or tears on the bloodsheets. *No!* Rub me bear, rub me
where teddy bear of out on the garbage pail from dirty fingers, dirty
girl fingers and juice tears. Squeezed by the baker in baby powder.
I'm rolled in flowers and batter round the rim of the licking bowl. A
good little girl in frills and soiled doilies. Scuff my shoes in the
gravel pit, up through a stomach of acid pie baked with love served
with a smack and a whack.

I am not here no I am not here. *Crank.*

Mixed up in the blender, bender baby cries funnelly. Something is
empty and burning in the. Smell the black cloud turn gray, see oven
smoke smiles disappear in the shatter song of speech. Where did
garden grub fingers go. They are falling asleep already, the garden
drops. An alarm sounds like. Unlike.

Slip through grub fingers, can't catch me, I'm mercury. Quick as a
bubble pop black all over your face. And you can't wipe me off your
lips. I'm popping. I'm spreading and bleeding all over your
conscience. You are dreaming.

Go away ugly man. Go away.

freeze

some people ride life's orgasm
always expecting
the second coming

perhaps i am simply frigid
an impotent voyeur
dizzy on a flask
of knowledge

margins of sky
close in on me
like a book folded
at sunrise

comptroller above
fastens buttons and
feathers to mountainous
lapels

winter knocks
and bites
my nipples

fish

38

do you etch your thoughts in bubbles
an ocean wave—does it feel like breeze
you fly like eagles through channels
in the liquid life you lead

do you read astronomy on seaweed
debate politics with sharks
your existence seems so simple
to a land dweller in the dark

drift

and if we did not have
feet
would we better understand
the clouds

imagination

wistfully his shoe
scuffed the carpet
mindless

his longing stretched
to China where
a fisherman gazed
at his empty net

wish I could be
like you, have such
a vivid imagination
he complained

his Siamese cat
hissed defiantly

I cringed
allergic to its lice,
oh,
dander

I pictured a thousand pikes
choked in their maws
while he spoke
he drowned me in
spit

I protested—

this is America
so surely you can

     buy someone else's

he finally shut up

the fisherman went home
with his empty fortune

eye language, 1984

what kind of name is that?

>   russian.

you don't look russian. are you
>   eskimo?

>   no. i'm not from alaska.

russian? that means you are
>   communist?

>   no, i'm not communist.
>   i'm american.

but russia is communist.

>   i'm russian orthodox.

orthodox? you are orthodox jew?
>   a russian jew?
>   is your family from odessa?

>   no.

you sure you're not a commie?

    [*squint*]

                i already told you—

you're chinese, aren't you! that's

    what you are! china is commie!

                i'm *NOT* chinese.

i ate chinese food once. chow mein.

    you look like those people there.

    are you related to charlie

    chan? [*squint*]

                no. he's chinese.

so who's chinese in your family? must be

    your mother. why do you have an

    italian last name? it's italian, right?

                uh huh.

you don't look italian. how did you get an

    italian last name? [*squint*]

    my mother is italian and nobody

    in my family looks like you you look

    funny how can you see out of those

                       ➤➤

eyes they are so small I can't see out
of eyes when I get them that tiny
[*squint*]

> i can see just fine.
> [*eyes roll up*]

i don't think so. no i don't think so.
you can't see, cuz I can't
see [*squint*] which way you're
looking right now!

> that's because you're
> squinting.

no, i don't believe you, you can't
see out of those eyes [*squint*]
how do you know english
anyway, do you eat with
chopsticks?

> i eat the same as you.

those chinese people at the
restaurant they ate with
chopsticks it's true! and you
must eat with chopsticks,
where'd you say you were
from? bangkok?
[*squint*]

> i already told you.

huh?

i'm american.
just like you.

no you're not! no way!
get away from me! liar!
you squinty-eyed people
are all liars!

pretense

some days I pretend
I'm a superstar
in jeans
a cap
old t-shirt
as if it were choice
to grunge around
walk my island of
pretend
I am   Incognito

yesterday I
played this

charade
me, attentive
audience

oh Eyes!
try not to see
it is a game

of no-show-tell
        of   who *gives* a flying
Eyes averted
                in this city of
                home sweet
Don't look at me
        please   Look at me
Don't look at me
        unless I want you
to see me

in Central Park
drowning in green

in Washington Square
baking on asphalt

in Times Square
gagging at Disney
cursing Giuliani   what he did

I huff like a 212-er
pissed to have
to add 4 more digits
for local calls

angry angled
elbow of hand
on hip

dammit!
why didn't anyone
let me know
        my fly was open

coins

48

panhandler in
camouflage
approaches
in slow pace of
jingle jangle

spare any change?

I look away
reminded, disgusted
how attached
I am to my pockets

did his cup once
hold coffee? I realize
my mouth is dry

I refuse to buy
water

I walk by

street vendors
        charge more
        on weekends
I am no tourist!

        do I look like one?

I get pissed

*HEY! didn't we kill
all you gooks in 'Nam?*

face red

all this to save
a quarter

quitter

he got skin flapping in his throat
and flap skinning up his nose
sleeping on the nob driving witted
he is the yellow flit. bit o' flit to
light his cigarette. tax it up to broke.
one pack go in choke. hack. crumble beads
out the back. box. mark in it. grind. smoke'll
toke'll. tuck a token buy'n a ride
past recovery. when cold can't
keep him warm. coats of why. as.
words don't cut it.

off the page

yellow cabs squawk corners in fury of hurry
steel shoulders spin on axis
pages skimmed in whirs, blurs,
exhaust fumes vein beneath a begrudging sun

critics remain flippant, spit in the manuscript trash pail
coffee gathers frost while iron arms tick
they all ask: where is the next Poe, Dickenson, Pound?

ballet instructor taps her spindly foot—*nyet! nyet!*
where is the next Baryshnikov! Pavlova! Danilova!
did I starve all my life to remain so empty *still?*

battered lady carries woes to a shelter
there is a man back home brandishing a loaded gun
tomorrow she'll return to him: lead bullets
sell cheaper than bread

actor-cum-waiter drops the second basket down, *Plop!*
two diners look up, aghast, already full from
a pitcher of tap and now more free rolls
back to the register, he calculates,
twenty per cent of nothing is still nothing

cabbies shoot for their stars with fenders,
urban organists play gas pedals and brakes
in tempo to traffic lights and pedestrians
circular symphonies rise above indifferent city streets
then fall and crack the blistered soul of asphalt

la vecindad donde vivo

cocks crowing at 5AM
life in Spanish Harlem
wake-up call to nocturne
music of garbage trucks
clashing against the salsa
beating through open windows
reaching happiness through
rhythm since food stamps
can't pay for Prozac

I imagine the projects
across the street as luxury
hi-rise Trump Towers
without the tacky adornments
and plastic women
revolving through glass doors,
transparent, and translucent
as the color of their skin

the welcome call of
the neighborhood hombres
gave me a new nombre
chinita, chinita,
through gold-tooth smiles
since I, too, am pobrecita

playing dominos on cracked sidewalks
wet from the makeshift carwashes
courtesy of New York City
fire hydrants used to cool off
overheated children

splashing, laughing with life,
for life, at life,

getting by and getting along
as represented by
the fusion of yellow rice and
egg foo yong
aromas drifting out of
takeout joints next to
bodegas that sell everything
from radios and GI Joes
to middle eastern nan and
Goya Sazón con azafrán

centenarian

54

his woodgrained face
of aged cork   dry wine
poured forth from lips   crimson
cranberry twinkle and
cherry blossom eyebrows
crinkled just so   almost sour-sweet
taste of afternoon   strokes
knobby knuckles   on park bench
holding on for dear life, brace
against sharp young blades
ripping by gee! whiz, peripheral
blurs an overindulgent second
of exploding sparrow branches
intoxicating him again
with whiplash

55

morning rush

56

the lady falls in
plops herself
next to me
as I was in mid-
morn dream
she squeezes in
presses up
expands her ham
thighs with a sigh
annoyed to rub
so intimately with a
no-face-name she
shoulders a resentful
flow to tram into
her linger of wake
my thigh not her lover's
she spooned this
morning & tries to
recreate the moment
inside her eyelids
they flutter above
her cheeks crash
and burn into wisps
of mustard-in-coffee
shade locks so very

sex-mess-look
glorious display of
smugness stapled
to her scalp her bo-
som her insides of
labia and perfectly
manicured nails dug
into palms, wishing
it were already time
to go home

uptown six

moments leak
between them
       they
only slightly
shift
from the ones
before

coats hang in
continental
drifts   noses
arrow down
to socks
       laps
cinched
       belts

when she
flurries in
wind beneath
    chins
       whirl
    snowflakes
melt away
    bemused
stares
knocked from

     Dr. Zizmore's
post—
          pimpled
face.
this.
     winter
swells
chrome curves
outward
             from her
legs
drawn by
direct
     connection
to the
equator

slide a
telescope
   over   everyone's
land bodies

                in orbit
   we all shift
together

top stair of exit

she inhales   puffy lips, pouty
    on a corner   a   l o n g   t h o u g h t
through a cigarette   paper wrapped round
an idea
or   an attitude of
                 an idea   draws me in
for a blink   into her
  tube   her throat   her belly
and   back   unsteady
    I teeter, reassembled in
my simple shoes   shiny
              shocks, manta sting rays
of sunlight   crash and bomb
onto my head   space
   through ozone
cata
         pult
                              ed
         [coughed] through
galactic lungs

I rest
weary of the
                 1. thought
                 2. heat
                 3. hunger

risen amidst oatmeal waves
   of commuters spilt
and swallowed
         by geometric planes

petals

61

when love turns
to a question mark,
to when
suddenly,
question marks
turn the order
of all things

breakfast

when ovaries pop
i feel another
unscrambled eye drop,
ablaze

i don't eat
unfertilized animals!

who cares?
mother hen
clucks with forked
disapproval

bacon and grill
hiss in chorus at me,
post-coital fashion

so do you want to send it back
she booms
there are children starving
where you came from

where i came from?
i ponder the yellow center
and its white border
of teeth poised to snap

even the juice glass
sweats

no, it's ok, i'll keep it

sharp tongs pierce
sunshine,
such bleeding always runs
in circles

ad infinitum

64

I have flowed in and out of you infinite times
In another reality we are indistinguishable
Prejudices aside
The flesh we wear, a barrier we carry
Created by human folly
Call it Experience
Out of a single possibility

five minutes til...

65

firestorm rages across
continent's breast
while poverty hovers

silver dollar moons
glisten in the cosmic
oil spill of space

obsolete currency
churns out in lieu of
paper flags

burns and melts
for the weight
of bullets

faces stare,
bloodsmears
behind paper bars

feet that have already
been cut like wheat
from soil
irrigate new furrows
pushed by ink
through an adopted land, again
signing its supplicants away

traversing a cavern's maw,
nine months or not,
the burden of time
pulls apart brittle seams
five minutes til midnight

for Samira

where across a
continent of fables

one mouse can possess
the courage of a lion

you, small creature
have ridden the waves

the tournantes failed
to silence you

you cast bottle out
an unrelenting ocean

your message can
not drown   it has

cut glass beneath feet
walked water

and more shall carry
your song to freedom

backwash

I sit astride myself
upon a semi seat of maybe—
five toes pointed toward a future
five curled from the past
and between the heels
a pumice heap of soil

crying down its hem
for recollection
over the arches of yesterday
it always yearns

another turn in the
life cycle; we pedal back up
the steep hill long after we've farewelled
that long distant aunt, farther
and faster into the distance
drinking the wind as water,
our legs awash in lactic nostalgia

the armies will stomp after it
once more, indignant
in line,
tired of the narrow paths
of overgrown hedges of time;
with scythes they will
arrest their periodic flow,
coagulate their cries
thundered against
missile and fire;

attempt to arrest the future
with new age medicine
or ointment to
clear nostrils of
the hemorrhaged stench
of bitter reminiscences

where once we danced
in the floodlight,
such greatness will
find a new home in history;
and all the daughters
I shall not bear
whose voices
I shall not hear
will cry through what
remaining sons

have not lost as
we
become lost
to find ourselves again
led astray
the foghorn of home still calling
to us

beyond a sun where
the corners of my lips
once visited

fashionably late

.....sugar and spice

post saturday night party
lips mat with fragrance
of his want. swelled, and
a rose   to her lips
so beautiful as she
lies still   silently now,

.....and all that's nice

for her want, broken
empty vessel, ming dynasty-type
victimised somewhat- vogue-like
bites the   high time
prime time   cameo appearance
on CNN:

.....that's what

pendulum swung
between thighs, an anchor
narration how a perp's
need took swipes

                              .....little girls are made of

inside nightly news
reports, spoken in chips
of concrete paid by sponsors
advertising *"how to get a
beautiful body in five minutes"*

                              .....a spoonful of sugar

the anchor drops
rolling lines, straight/rigid
technical   [-ly]
more smiles pretty for
Johnny-cum-lately
quicksnapshots
backdrop of red silk drapes
of ambulance sirens arcing thru
winter gray

                       .....makes the medicine go down

down deep sinks   second pendulum
scooping out   [editing out]
~~shriveled ovaries [slashed out]~~
offensive material

                              .....medicine go down

                                        ➤➤

mothers at home teach daughters—

sit pretty and smile

with legs crossed;

don't spread

a negative reputation

.....what are little boys made of

too many smiles cause wrinkles
fault lines cause earthquakes
science books teach, she forgot
but remembered

.....snakes and snails

too much intelligence is a turnoff

intelligence is a turnoff

don't be a showoff

stupid girl

how can you ever

get a man

like that

.....and puppy dog tails that's what

dance and be pretty

don't speak, not a whisper

don't touch don't move

don't don't don't don'tdon't*don't*

don't baby oh *baby*

just lie still, legs closed,

legs open, open wide, smile

.....little boys are

& be still for the camera

say *cheese* you are happy

for mama, for papa

for everyone but you

baby, baby dead

stay just like that / forever

you ~~ng & fragile like a nestling~~ [cliché]

fallen away now from home   so beautiful

you are. in slices   so pearly white / and /

.....made of

slender / beautiful bones // perfectly

          / ~~exhumed.~~ / perfumed.

Mr. Bones

breathing flesh I
cannot love it, no
cannot, and
the skeleton in the corner
agrees, he
is dressed with a white beard
a flowered dress hung on its bones
I have hung him, and on him, dearly:
>   *oh my darling*
>   *only you can reach through*
>   *these hollow ribs of mine*
his silent grin nods
an illusion of a flickering incandescent light
as if he could protest
given the choice

one cannot emasculate a man
who has no penis
one cannot hurt a man
who has no heart
one cannot fight a man
who possesses no muscles
or mouthful
or ego

Jack was so good oh he
would have shared his townhouse with me
but an enclosed garden and
four floors not barely enough to escape
the grasp of his fleshy fingers
or reaching heart grip tight as a pitbull jaw
aiming for mine (wherever it may have gone to then)

no divorce paper could have been
strong enough to collapse
the bridge of permanent ink linking
his name on the same page as mine
for it is just paper
and paper merely cuts: it does not kill
oh yes, he loved me
oh yes, he breathed me
oh yes, he wished to possess my everything
but
I had not yet discovered the everything
of me I could give

and David was the same (all three of them)
and Tom was the same
and Joe was the same
unlike this silent fellow who is wise—
already passed through the inhuman torment of
rigor mortis and decay—
he understands this pain of clung flesh
and the heat of its loss

oh Mr. Bones I will eventually
wither away like you
as you wait for me:
          you are eternally patient
amused by my antics
you bear no grudges
you do not expect compromise
for you cannot compromise
for you are no hypocrite
and you are eternally amused
by all my human follies
I wear inside and out
simply by biological default

I forgive you your smile
a solitary comedic audience to my living error
on a stage where I cannot reconcile
the infinite shades of gray
the messy stuff which rests in my cranium
and the moving branches of
similar—but not enough so
or maybe too much so?—minds of others
where my kite thoughts get caught
in their twigs, and I am left dangled without rescue
while you watch, knowing eventually
my breath will blow away
and we shall dance in the sky together

Intimacy

About the Author

Anyssa Kim is a poet, writer, self-taught visual artist and performance artist, and classically trained violinist. She plays regularly with the New York Repertory Orchestra, has been on stage performing her own monologues at the Westbeth Theater and Nuyorican Poets Café theater, has been invited to read short stories and poetry at Mixta Gallery, A Gathering of the Tribes, Bowery Poetry Club and Cornelia Street Café, and has read at universities such as Pace University Law School, Sarah Lawrence College, and Fordham University. She has poetry included in the tenth issue of *A Gathering of the Tribes* magazine.

Anyssa Kim was born in Seoul, Korea and was adopted and raised in the suburban town of Westbury, Long Island. She managed to escape, and has lived on her own in New York City for over a decade.